Rejuvenation:
Innocent Until Proven Guilty

Poetry By

Stacey Barlow

Rejuvenation: Innocent Until Proven Guilty
By: Stacey Barlow

Cover design by: Martha Gonzales
Last picture on the inside: by Aaron Ellies
Cover created by: Anelda L. Attaway
Logo designs by: Andre M. Saunders and Leroy Grayson
Editor: Jazzy Kitty Publishing

© 2005 Stacey Barlow TXu1—273--977

ISBN 978-0-9830548-8-7
Library of Congress Control Number: 2011945864

All rights reserved. This book is protected under the copyright laws of the United States of America. This book may not be copied or reprinted for commercial gain or profit. The use of short quotations or occasional page copying for personal or group study is permitted and encouraged. Permission will be granted upon request.

For Worldwide Distribution. Printed in the United States of America. Published by Jazzy Kitty Greetings Marketing & Publishing, LLC dba Jazzy Kitty Publishing. Utilizing Microsoft Publishing Software.

ACKNOWLEDGMENTS

Thank you to the One and Only who has given me life and life abundantly--I love you, my Heavenly Father.

To My Friends: There are too many to name old and new so, I thank you in advance.

To the Authors: To the ones I have grown to love and know as friends. . .You are very special to me.

To My Family: Thank you all once again for your love and support.

Special Thanks: To the company that put in such long hours to get things right--Thank you from the bottom of my heart.

Very Special Thanks: To the Janet Jackson fan club friends; without you, my words could not be expressed in the way that they needed to be. Thank you for letting me into your world. This one is for you. . .

Extra special thanks: To Lucky 7 (for the inspiration given to continue)

Life is worthless without structure and substance: to six forces that gave me a voice in different ways. Randy Bolden, Carliest Daniels, Joe D. Hubbard, Darrick Hunter, Kendrick Smith, and Davie White~~I love you.

To the women of character whom are my backbone: Juanita Barlow, Djuna Blackmon, Gina Couch (For helping me to step out on faith), Rene Daniels, Sarah Henderson, DeAna Smith, Kathy Vaughn and the late Angela Perry (April 24, 1967-December 5, 2011).

To the ones who make me smile: KiAna D. and Kyron J. Smith.

DEDICATIONS

To my inner selves, Epiphany Moon, Honey Rainn and Dark Phoenix.

For those who stand up for what they believe in regardless of what someone else has said. Keep your heads up and going against the grain.

In loving memory of LaShawn Hendricks.

Life is too short to be angry "just breathe. . .and let it go."
--Lisa "Left Eye" Lopes

"The world needs to hear what you have to say. The last word has not been spoken."--Bea Richards

In loving memory of Donald P. Haynes 1963-2010.

In loving memory of Carlin "Oz" Johnson August 8, 1975-March 14, 2011.

{You know when your smile is bigger than the problems you face, God had a hand in it~I love you and will miss you from the bottom up.}

--Joe D. Hubbard

June 15, 1956~March 22, 2011 {I thank God for sending you my way. Not just "my" way but, others as well; and I'm sure that "the choir" also known as "your other children" feel the same. For me, you dedicated 33 years of your blood, sweat and tears to show and teach us the love of God. You instilled in us that if you are not singing from the heart and meaning it, that our singing is in vain~I get that now. You will always be "The Man" to me . . .}

Rejuvenation: Innocent Until Proven Guilty

By: Stacey Barlow

TABLE OF CONTENTS

INTRODUCTION i
    Carrousel 01
    Reflections 04
    Understand 07
    Chills 09
    Letter To My Editor 11
    Version 14
    Say Yes (Part II) 16
    Can I Have A Taste (of You?) 18
    Catchy Tune 22
    Heart Be Still 26
    Your Missing Rib 29
    Nubian King 31
    Subliminally/Eyes/The Two of Them 34
    Blue Diamond 35
    Inside 38
    Let The Truth Be Known 39
    Unshelter Me 42
    Drastic Overload 45
    Weak Limit 48
    Dumb 51
    Quiet Reverence 53
    Father Dream 54
    Soul Searching 55
    Eternal Friendship 58

TABLE OF CONTENTS

Have You Given Thanks Today? 60
Repetition 63
Mountain 65
Not A Broken Dream 67
Learning 69
Ms. Classified 70
My Village 73
Ocean's Tears 75
Second Infinity 77
Sister on the Rise (The Answer) 78
Walk in My Shoes 81
Rejuvenation 83
Why I Support RAINN 84
Real Women/Fake Men 85
Deliver Me 90
Dangerous Thoughts 91
Wish You Were Here (2 Pac) 93
But God (Ice Berry Chronicles) 95
Bullet Proof 98
Feeling The Pain (Ice Berry Second Chronicles) 100
Carry On 102
Green-Eyed Devil 104
Lipstick On Collar (Ask Me) 106
Lipstick On Collar (Part II) 110
Conversation 115

TABLE OF CONTENTS

Guess Who's	60
Conference Call	125
Conclusion	128
The End	136
Tick Tick Boom (Wooosah Moment)	139
What Did I Say?	142
Shock To The System	144
Rejuvenation	146
Addiction	148
Punany Ritual	150
This Piece Does Not Belong To You	151
Nine Lives	154
About the Author	157

INTRODUCTION

Dear Reader:

What you are about to witness is a most profound journey to the other side of relationships when one person in a relationship wants things one way when in reality, the other individual involved does not reciprocate the same type of feelings. This can become the most dangerous yet provoking kind of relationship ever known to man.

Rejuvenation: Innocent Until Proven Guilty is a fact of life to most people and a fantasy for some. Women can love hard and it is said that men are incapable of loving. This type of love can possibly lead to death if not taken precautions the correct way. Through words of poetry, you will find, joy, pain, happiness and strength and lead you away from the dangers of obsession. Men can love just as hard.

Rejuvenation: Innocent Until Proven Guilty is an in-depth look at a deeper side of love that has a true beauty as well. It's all right to love…it's not all right to love someone to death. Stop the madness.

Stacey

REJUVENATION: INNOCENT UNTIL PROVEN GUILTY

Stacey Barlow

CARROUSEL

A vision of a Rainbow

With a lasting Silhouette

Of bursting Flavor

Find alas. . .

A Spirit after Soul Searching

Only one body can Savor.

Before a taste of Honey

A Casual Look beyond

The eyes of a Scheme

Demanding the on set

Of a Sunset

Partly close eyes Wishing of a Dream.

Glancing upward to the Stars

And they ONLY understand

REJUVENATION: INNOCENT UNTIL PROVEN GUILTY

Stacey Barlow

A Woman's Tears

Flowing downward

Forever streaming

Carelessly beyond her Years.

High as the Quarter Moon,

Darker as the Darkest Skies

Forget in the back of my mind

Showing Love Denies.

I ain't feeling you

Deep in thought around my Head

Hoping that I'm wrong too

Stop being with you Instead.

Rewind to the Future,

Fast forward to the Past

Stuck in the NOW

REJUVENATION: INNOCENT UNTIL PROVEN GUILTY

Stacey Barlow

Fearing it's hard To Let Go
Common sense will show you how.

Strong as an Amazon,
Smooth as a River
Back to my Rainbow again
With a Silhouette of Bursting Flavor.

Girl, I am not,
A woman Born of one
Fearless from the Beginning
Without a Pro or a Con.

With or without a Better Half
Goddesses can EXCEL
I am known to be one
On a Poet's Dream
Of a Carrousel.

REJUVENATION: INNOCENT UNTIL PROVEN GUILTY

Stacey Barlow

REFLECTIONS

My Love,

Seeing you is like a Breath of Fresh Air

You came to me when I was Lonely

You're the ONLY ONE who seemed to Care

You are my Divine Sun

I am your Challenged Moon

Shine your Love Light Shine

Within a Dark Filled Room.

Silver Shadow on a Golden Cloud

Please take me away

I'm feeling the Air you Breathe

Don't go, PLEASE STAY!

Eyes all a Glow with skies Purple Pink

My Sun has gone down

It's time to fill my Glass and Rethink.

REJUVENATION: INNOCENT UNTIL PROVEN GUILTY

Stacey Barlow

Warmth Lost and Love gained
Showered blessings bring the Rain
I am the Moon that makes his Night
He is My Sun to give me Light.

He sees what I see--
I'm all he's worth
I'm his Sun, his Moon, his Cipher,
And his Earth.

We rotate on an axis with the Planets
Giving us a Direct Connection
Therefore, he is still My Earth
My Moon, My Cipher, My Sun.

As seen through the Eyes of a Child

I've Learned to Like Myself
I'm Older now. . .
Learning to Love Myself

REJUVENATION: INNOCENT UNTIL PROVEN GUILTY

Stacey Barlow

Differentiate the Parts of My Soul
I can't stop Fighting
I'm beginning to Show. . .
My TRUE colors
Time to STOP Hiding.

Heaven help me if I lose My Sun
Heaven help him if he lost His Moon
My Sun is Guiding me
To come out of My Shell
And not a moment too soon.

Things are taken to Heart
And things to know
These are the things to Remember. . .
My Reflections in the Window.

REJUVENATION: INNOCENT UNTIL PROVEN GUILTY

Stacey Barlow

UNDERSTAND

I never understood what happened between
YOU AND ME

Days would go by and I'd think
He's a Wonderful Guy. . .
Deep in my Heart
I wanted us to be
Something that most people aren't
HAPPY

Honestly, you caused me "some" Pain
I choose to forget
What happened Before
NO LESS -- NO MORE

Anything's possible, you must know
With anything possible: I LOVE YOU SO

REJUVENATION: INNOCENT UNTIL PROVEN GUILTY

Stacey Barlow

Given the time and place:

I Want you

Need you

Long for you

Miss you

Ache for you

I Crave for the Sweet Kiss and Tenderness

Oh! How things could be

I Love You With All My Heart

I'd love for you to have a chance. . .

TO LOVE ME.

REJUVENATION: INNOCENT UNTIL PROVEN GUILTY

Stacey Barlow

CHILLS

If it takes two
Then why am I alone?
Things I need to do
About things I have known

Cream, Scream, Ice, Holler,
Melted Sun. . .
Squeezing like a Dog's Collar
I AIN'T the One.

Days have Gone by
With Minds Drained
Often figure why
Standing in the Rain.

Throb, Pound in and out,
Bodies turning

REJUVENATION: INNOCENT UNTIL PROVEN GUILTY

Stacey Barlow

What's it all about?

Heart is Yearning.

Four corners of the mind

SET ME FREE

I desire to be your kind

INFINITY.

REJUVENATION: INNOCENT UNTIL PROVEN GUILTY

Stacey Barlow

LETTER TO THE EDITOR

Dear Editor:

I was hoping you could help me find my Soul Mate
He lives in a different Time Zone and State.

I've spoken with him several times to find that
I think he Likes me as well
But with the Distance in the way
All I can do is send E-mail.

My Heart aches because I Miss him So Much
Just for the Sound of his Voice
Or someday, a Soft Touch.

I'm delighted to have gotten to know him
In a short period of time
And in My Heart, I know that he's Mine.

REJUVENATION: INNOCENT UNTIL PROVEN GUILTY

Stacey Barlow

Maybe that's a bit Pushy and I do Apologize
For being so forward and his words
Which brought Tears to my Eyes.

I lay in my bed at night. . .
Pillows wet with tears

All I asked is to be given another Chance by him
To Grow Old with him through the years.
I've tossed and turned, wrinkling my sheets
Seems like never to sleep again
Knowing that in my heart,
There is ONLY one man.

You should have seen my Face, Cheeks swollen
And my Eyes blood shot red
That's from crying since Sunday
My body feels Numb, almost Dead.

REJUVENATION: INNOCENT UNTIL PROVEN GUILTY

Stacey Barlow

My Knees are weak

And my Fingers refuse to write

Just Hoping and Praying

For his Call one night.

I don't know if you could help. . .

I just needed to get it off my chest

Maybe then I could stop crying

And get a good night's rest.

The only thing is that I think of him constantly

I close my eyes at night

And it's him I see

In my heart

I feel that it needs to be

Dear Editor,

    I desire him to be my soul mate

Sincerely,

Me

REJUVENATION: INNOCENT UNTIL PROVEN GUILTY

Stacey Barlow

VISION

He stepped highly into my Dreams where. . .

I was only being left behind by

The Smell of his words I can only

Imagine what it would be like if. . .

He touched me Once and I touched him Twice

Our bodies' Melted with each Vibration

From the sound of our Heartbeats.

There was no Love made

Just eye contact

Don't you understand?

I Breathe this man

I inhaled him only to fill

My lungs with the sweet Essence

Of his Cool Waters trickling

REJUVENATION: INNOCENT UNTIL PROVEN GUILTY

Stacey Barlow

Down the side of my mouth and then. . .
And then, and then. . .
I Exhaled him only
To capture him in the Palm of my Hand
And NEVER let him go

You see,
He is the Ice to my Fire
That my Spirit, Mind, and Body needs

REJUVENATION: INNOCENT UNTIL PROVEN GUILTY

Stacey Barlow

SAY YES (PART II)

Tonight let us close the doors and open our minds

To a world of color that no one else will know but us

I can feel the Vibrations of your hands not even

Touching my skin as you make me So, So, So. . .

My mind drifts to your mind just to tell you

That I am only human

Your eyes burn into my Soul

Like a Moth to a Flame

Burned by the Fire

I can't contain it

Won't Let Go of it

Can you Feel it?

Can you hear it?

My Heart Whispering for you

To come to me. . .

REJUVENATION: INNOCENT UNTIL PROVEN GUILTY

Stacey Barlow

In a Strong Embrace
And when you do,
I'll be there with Open Arms
To comfort you with my Mind

Right there, Right there, Right there. . .
Ahhhhhhh, did you feel it like I just did?

I can't contain it
It's so good
I want to Frame it
I think I've Named it, Claimed it
It's Mine, it's Yours, it's Ours.

You make me So, So, So, So. . .
Just for a moment, and in a time
Will you say YES?

REJUVENATION: INNOCENT UNTIL PROVEN GUILTY

Stacey Barlow

CAN I HAVE A TASTE (OF YOU)?

CAN I HAVE A TASTE OF YOU. . .
In the Midnight hour?
Like Chocolate covered Strawberries
Draped on a table of Flowers.

CAN I HAVE A TASTE OF YOU. . .
During the Noonday?

Where no one can bother us
Phone's off the hook
With the doors locked

I'm pheenin' for that TASTE OF YOU
During a cold shower/warm bath with
Scented Candles
I am a bit of a Romantic
ONE TASTE is enough for me to handle

REJUVENATION: INNOCENT UNTIL PROVEN GUILTY

Stacey Barlow

CAN I HAVE A TASTE OF YOU, your honey?

In the Morning time
Uh-uh don't get out of bed just yet
I want to make you all mine
Soaking wet, Dripping with Sweat
Delight my senses and yours
While TASTING YOU on the ocean shores.

I thought I had that TASTE OF YOU when you
Called that evening just to say Good Night
Ohhh how my body Yearned for yours
My body Aches for the Passion inside
So well, I thought I seen the Light.

Can I take you in and engulf you like my
Favorite piece of Candy?
Aww...My scope...I didn't mean to call you Randy.

REJUVENATION: INNOCENT UNTIL PROVEN GUILTY

Stacey Barlow

That's not your name, and I know this

But just let me TASTE YOU. . .

Before you're Dismissed.

CAN I HAVE A TASTE OF YOU. . .

Before you go to work?

That will take the pressure off a long day

(Jerk)

CAN I HAVE A TASTE OF YOU. . .

At your Lunch hour

Nibble on you like a sandwich?

I've had my Breakfast; Lunch and Dinner. . .

You get the hint.

I need a Taste, I want a Taste. . .

CAN I HAVE A TASTE?

I'm pheenin' for it now

REJUVENATION: INNOCENT UNTIL PROVEN GUILTY

Stacey Barlow

I'll be your Teacher this time
And you will Learn how
To Taste the Essence of my being
And much time you cannot waste
Like Cream to my Chocolate
CAN I HAVE A TASTE?

Subliminally,
I take you where I want you
To take me at Night

REJUVENATION: INNOCENT UNTIL PROVEN GUILTY

Stacey Barlow

CATCHY TUNE

He led me to the bedroom with a simple Kiss
He let me taste his sweet skin
In between his Thighs like this.

He let me climb that Mountain;
I've wanted to climb
Once inside me,
I knew he was mine.

I closed my eyes to feel what was inside
He put an arch in my back and said,
"Get ready, it's going to be a bumpy ride."

No words were spoken into the night
As we rode six hours straight
Damn! It's only 12 am, and that's not late.

REJUVENATION: INNOCENT UNTIL PROVEN GUILTY

Stacey Barlow

I rose up slowly,
And went down the same
The look on his face told me that he Came.

"Stay right there, and Kiss me Damn It!"
He went in deeper feeling in the spots of my Clit.

I was in control of this game
Never to stop teasing this man
I called mine Insane.

All I wanted to do was give him some
Add then all he wanted to do. . .
Was make me Cum for him.

I did several times,
And then some more
The bed started vibrating and fell to the floor.

REJUVENATION: INNOCENT UNTIL PROVEN GUILTY

Stacey Barlow

He looked at me with those greyish-brown eyes
And said, "I wanna Fuck you!"
And I let him do what he want to.

He's on top, Licking that spot
As he continued to go down
To make sure he had A Lot.

Oh, magical tongue work your magic Boo
He came up for me to taste
And it tasted Sweet too.

He went down to please me, One more time
He made me Cum harder, and he liked it
So, I knew he was Mine.

The tempo calmed while he held me. . .
As I vibrated

REJUVENATION: INNOCENT UNTIL PROVEN GUILTY

Stacey Barlow

I wrapped my arms around him
Like I did when we dated.

I took care of every inch the other woman Missed
I rocked him so good; I made him forget
Everyone on his List.

I kid you not
Yes, I'm that good and there is nothing to Fear
The catchy tune
I'm trying to get you to Hear.

REJUVENATION: INNOCENT UNTIL PROVEN GUILTY

Stacey Barlow

HEART BE STILL

I was on fire for his Soul
Before he put out the flame
He said things that were very Cold

Harsh to my Spirit
Put my heart to Shame
Only knew him for a moment

Before he said, "Breathe"
My Heart listens intensely
My Soul floated to the Skies
So far away you wouldn't Believe

The first sound of Hello
Made my Ears Ring
It sounded like music
To a song I wanted to Sing

REJUVENATION: INNOCENT UNTIL PROVEN GUILTY

Stacey Barlow

I was Vibing him
And he was Vibing me
Was I the one that was Blind?
Was I the one that Could See?

If he's out there Listening
I only hope that you find it in your heart
To Forgive
In the meantime,
I'll tell my Heart to be Still.

Maybe I invaded your Privacy
Or that I entered the Wrong Territory

I never meant to anger your Spirit
Because you're Not really blind
I know you can see

REJUVENATION: INNOCENT UNTIL PROVEN GUILTY

Stacey Barlow

If you are such a man
Who has a forgiving Heart

I'll be glad to have you as a friend
I guess what I'm asking. . .
IS THAT WE CAN START AGAIN?

REJUVENATION: INNOCENT UNTIL PROVEN GUILTY

Stacey Barlow

YOUR MISSING RIB

When you walked by me there was a pain in your side
I know you felt the pain you could have denied.

You stepped to me and boldly stated
Your Name, Number and Invitation
AND POLITELY WAITED.

Keeper of the field and shepherd of the flock
If you desire the door to be open, Knock.
Disciple of Jesus, fisherman of the sea
Whatever you want in life. . .
IT SHALL BE.

The pain is still there
Let me Heal it for you
With Jesus at the head
THERE IS NOTHING WE CAN'T DO.

REJUVENATION: INNOCENT UNTIL PROVEN GUILTY

Stacey Barlow

Please Kiss me with kisses of your mouth
For your Love is better than Wine
For I've seen No Other Man
AS BEAUTIFUL AND KIND.

I will seek him whom my Soul Loveth
I sought him, but I found him not
When he found me,
He was crowned in the day of gladness
IN HIS HEART.

Twin, I've written my Vision and made it Plain
Name it and Claim it, one Flesh,
NO MORE TWAIN.

Yes, selfish I am,
But I got dib
PRAYING TO BE YOUR MISSING RIB.

REJUVENATION: INNOCENT UNTIL PROVEN GUILTY

Stacey Barlow

NUBIAN KING

Lord have Mercy on my Soul

He is the one I want to Hold

Round and about the face his smile is so Bright

That wakes me with every Morning Light.

His skin is dark and smooth to the touch

If he only knew, I need him so much.

Soft and sweet to the taste

My tongue,

I will use it

If that be case

Don't make me lose it.

His hands, I'll kiss on all fingertips

Round and about the mouth

Otherwise known as Delightful lips.

REJUVENATION: INNOCENT UNTIL PROVEN GUILTY

Stacey Barlow

Oh! My Brotah, my wonderful King
Taking you for granted is Not my thing

You and I float to the Moon
Take me higher I don't want to
Come down Too Soon.

Bring me down slowly now
With your strength of know how

Over the Seas of Love
Across the Ocean Wave
We'll close our eyes to behave.

My beautiful Brotah,
My Nubian Brotah, come into my Dream
And make me flow like an easy Stream
And I'll know there is no other.

REJUVENATION: INNOCENT UNTIL PROVEN GUILTY

Stacey Barlow

We have done the forbidden thing

Lord have Mercy on my Soul

But it feels good my Nubian King

He's the One I want to Hold.

REJUVENATION: INNOCENT UNTIL PROVEN GUILTY

Stacey Barlow

SUBLIMINALLY

Subliminally
I take you where I want you
To take me at Night.

Eyes to Love is to See
To See is to Carry Smiles
And to Smile is Joy.

Para amar deberá ver
para ver deberá llevar las sonrisas
y a sonrisas es la alegría

The Two of Them

If I ask him soon
Will he say YES to Love me
Or will he say NO?

REJUVENATION: INNOCENT UNTIL PROVEN GUILTY

Stacey Barlow

BLUE DIAMOND

What I want for Christmas is a Jewel
The rarest of its kind
On that sits atop of my finger
A Blue Diamond comes to mind.

It's not much
But, It's something I Desire
Do you have the money for it?
Uh huh, I thought so . . . LIAR!
Not white nor gold
Blue . . .
I'm just asking
Can I get it from you?

This Jewel is Me in every way
This Jewel describes without words
To say

REJUVENATION: INNOCENT UNTIL PROVEN GUILTY

Stacey Barlow

A delicate piece

One that sits on top

Blue . . .It shall linger.

Blue diamond, Oh

How I wish for you

One that sits atop of my finger

A single Jewel will do.

A Jewel that everyone can see

A Jewel that also describes . . .Me

A Jewel in a rare form with no sound

A Jewel like no other that can't be found.

For Christmas, I want a JEWEL

That sits on top of my finger which describes Me

Rare, Beautiful, and Safe to keep

Infinity times three.

REJUVENATION: INNOCENT UNTIL PROVEN GUILTY

Stacey Barlow

I want a JEWEL that everyone can see

One question the JEWEL asks:

Can you afford me?

REJUVENATION: INNOCENT UNTIL PROVEN GUILTY

Stacey Barlow

INSIDE

I want you to Breathe

Every word into my

Mouth from yours as if

It were your last time to Speak

REJUVENATION: INNOCENT UNTIL PROVEN GUILTY

Stacey Barlow

LET THE TRUTH BE KNOWN

Has there ever come a time in your life
Where you wanted something so bad
That once you've turned around. . .
That piece of Gold was gone

What's that line again?
LET THE TRUTH BE KNOWN.

Needing to step back and Reevaluate
The prospects that have gone by
Also, leaving you all Alone

What's that line again?
LET THE TRUTH BE KNOWN.

At least now I can look back over my Life
And Not Cry

REJUVENATION: INNOCENT UNTIL PROVEN GUILTY

Stacey Barlow

But Laugh at the silliest things
That has gone on

Oh! What's that line again?
LET THE TRUTH BE KNOWN.

Take one look into my Eyes
For they are the mirrors to my Soul
I've planted my Seeds
And still they haven't Grown
I'm still waiting for that special Someone

What's that line again?
LET THE TRUTH BE KNOWN.

What is the truth?

It lies in all of us

REJUVENATION: INNOCENT UNTIL PROVEN GUILTY

Stacey Barlow

Only you can answer

And No Answer can be Wrong

My answers lies deep inside Me

What's that line again?

LET THE TRUTH BE KNOWN.

And the truth is. . .

REJUVENATION: INNOCENT UNTIL PROVEN GUILTY

Stacey Barlow

UNSHELTER ME

Clouded by my own Ignorance,

I saw Love in Eyes of others who were Different

In a stance

Far away, a few feet in mind

Not even half a Brain to see that Love can come

In all Shapes and Sizes

But, it's Wrong. . .

In a manner of speaking

If I just wanted to be myself

Instead of hiding

In tall grass where Love Grow

Weeds and Thorns

That pricks the finger. . .

Of the one you held that night

And burned the Stitches off your Forehead;

REJUVENATION: INNOCENT UNTIL PROVEN GUILTY

Stacey Barlow

We're only human
Just like those eyes that. . .
Pierce through the next
Heart you stand by.

Open Hands and Closed Minds bring. . .
Separation of Souls.

Lead me out of the idea that. . .
All is well

In the Wilderness,
When the Shelter is not clean.

I am Myself
I am I
I am You
I am She

REJUVENATION: INNOCENT UNTIL PROVEN GUILTY

Stacey Barlow

I am Fair

I am Love

I am Wind

I am Free

Unsheltered life...

Unshelter me.

REJUVENATION: INNOCENT UNTIL PROVEN GUILTY

Stacey Barlow

DRASTIC OVERLOAD

I couldn't wait for
Her fingers to touch My Skin
The night grew warm
With the Fall Wind.

And as dark erodes the sky and twilight begins
I tend to her skin as if that was the reasoning
Of my Birth

Electric explodes through my Body
As my Hand is raising her Skirt
Whispers telling her to prepare to be
Sexually Merked.

Closing my eyes. . .
I feel a sensation of lightning bolts succeeding
My Heart is telling me NO not now

REJUVENATION: INNOCENT UNTIL PROVEN GUILTY

Stacey Barlow

My Mouth is pleading
For the taste of Sweet revenge
In the midnight hour.

My Heart is exploding with temptation,
I Breathe the taste of you

Devouring everything on your body
From your ankles, to the sweat on your back

The shock I get from your lips,
The smoothness of your hips
The epitome in every sense of the word…
Goddess

Feeling you makes me want to cry out in Song
Saying how Sweet it is to take hold of the Nectar
You purge between the ever-loving Tongue

REJUVENATION: INNOCENT UNTIL PROVEN GUILTY

Stacey Barlow

Of speechless breath. . .
I Praise forever and a day

I'm the answer to your questions and everlasting lust
This is more than a bust,
Trust that I must feel your Touch.

My tongue gliding from North to South
The taste of your Sweet Juice
Everlasting in My Mouth.

REJUVENATION: INNOCENT UNTIL PROVEN GUILTY

Stacey Barlow

WEAK LIMIT

I find myself settling into you
Giving half of me to
Give back to you

The Love that I knew I could
Your mind everlasting thoughts of Fear
To the last drop of your Sweat
And your Tears
Devour the very essence your Spirit
You hold Near

Having strength of a Lion
With wisdom of the Dragon
And the Eyes of a bird in Flight

The Scars of Fear itself will keep you
If you don't put up a Fight.

REJUVENATION: INNOCENT UNTIL PROVEN GUILTY

Stacey Barlow

I find myself settling into you
Being comfortable in your
Words as you say. . .
"Excellent, Awesome, Prodigy,"

Whatever does that mean?
I know I'll Love you Faithfully

Creating a world without Degradation
And you Settling into Me
Will be a world of Excellence
For Both Eyes to See.

I want you to settle into me
And I settle into you
Protect us both from a world of
Fear and Hatred
That only Two Lovers can do.

REJUVENATION: INNOCENT UNTIL PROVEN GUILTY

Stacey Barlow

Let me make you Feel
The way you NEED to Feel

And be Comfortable with me at least
Where you'll bring power
To when my Soul is limited
And my Spirit is Weak.

REJUVENATION: INNOCENT UNTIL PROVEN GUILTY

Stacey Barlow

DUMB

Come here, let me whisper sum'in to ya
Shhh be quiet and don't tell no one
You made a fool out of yourself again
You sho' is Dumb.

How can you let this man you call a soldier
Leave you the way he did?
He told everybody else, but you
What does that tell you hun?
You made a fool out of yourself again
Chil' you sho' is Dumb.

He claims he wanted to be your friend
But the good word warns you of certain types
Didn't you read that one?
You made a fool out of yourself again
Sistah, you sho' is Dumb.

REJUVENATION: INNOCENT UNTIL PROVEN GUILTY

Stacey Barlow

Forgive him if you want, but that's on you
I can't help you none
I protected you from other people
And basically yourself
My love, you sho' is Dumb.

Forget is to make a mental note
Of the soldier who could be the fifth one
Shhh I ain't saying another word to you
But my queen
You sho' is Dumb.

REJUVENATION: INNOCENT UNTIL PROVEN GUILTY

Stacey Barlow

QUIET REVERENCE

Solace is

Quiet among the thieves

In the temple

REJUVENATION: INNOCENT UNTIL PROVEN GUILTY

Stacey Barlow

FATHER DREAM

They've fought for our Country

And stood on the Front Line

They've taken odd jobs

From working on the Railroad to Boot Shine.

They've been ridiculed

And spit on by their so called counterparts

Women must know,

They are the Loves of our Hearts

FATHER DREAM

God-Fearing men with a Smile

Or warm embrace

Even a Strong Voice that fills the air

To give Serenity to a place

FATHER DREAM

REJUVENATION: INNOCENT UNTIL PROVEN GUILTY

Stacey Barlow

A man who gives discipline

To become a Great and Mighty Nation

We know he is one of God's creations

FATHER DREAM

Fathers, hold your heads high

If it's the last thing you do

Now it's our turn

To take care of you

FATHER DREAM

REJUVENATION: INNOCENT UNTIL PROVEN GUILTY

Stacey Barlow

SOUL SEARCHING

If you ask me again,

I will say Nothing.

If you ask me from the Start

I will say Nothing.

If you question my Intelligence

I will go within.

If you refuse to ask,

I will Speak.

If you close my eyes

I will Breathe.

If you Breathe,

I will Move.

Having circles of Wisdom

That takes me within

My body is warm to the touch

Will you touch me?

If you touch me,

I will Freeze…And go within.

REJUVENATION: INNOCENT UNTIL PROVEN GUILTY

Stacey Barlow

Shadows of Meditation
Are heavy to the Heart
My eyes look like
Crystal glass
Hoping you will
Hope for me
I go within.

If you Stay,
I will Leave.
If you Leave,
I will say Nothing.
I will just go within.
Will you understand
If I open up to you?
If I Trust,
Will you lie?

I am always going to be Myself
Even if I still continue to Search.

REJUVENATION: INNOCENT UNTIL PROVEN GUILTY

Stacey Barlow

ETERNAL FRIENDSHIP

There have been times
When I needed a Friend
Someone to talk to
From Beginning to End.

Someone to be close to
To Comfort and Help
That someone would be
Your Inner Self.

Someone to be here
Through Thick and Thin
Someone to be friends with
Until the Very End.

Yet there are people in this world
That has No Friends

REJUVENATION: INNOCENT UNTIL PROVEN GUILTY

Stacey Barlow

Not one Boy or Girl

No close relation

Or next of Kin.

So the next time you meet a person

On the Street

Don't turn your back

Or his or her shoes

May Fit your Feet.

Try to make friends where ever you go

Friendship has no color

White,

Black,

Green,

Blue,

Or

Yellow

REJUVENATION: INNOCENT UNTIL PROVEN GUILTY

Stacey Barlow

HAVE YOU GIVEN THANKS TODAY?

Giving Thanks is a thing Learned
Learning is something that is Given
Given the opportunity to be Concerned
Concerned about the life you're Living.

Living while the day is Dawning
Dawning to see the sun Rise
Rise to see the sun Shining
Shining to know the glow in Eyes.

Eyes that says, "I LOVE YOU"
You to say it in Return
Return the love only you can Do
Do it to know what you can Earn.

Earn a Thought or Feeling thereof
Of a Price you didn't have to Pay

REJUVENATION: INNOCENT UNTIL PROVEN GUILTY

Stacey Barlow

Pay attention to those you Love
And ask yourself,
Have you Given Thanks Today?

Today is a day of Thanksgiving
Giving is an action that's Granted
Granted is a prize as you are Living.

Living is breath you have Chanted
Chanted are sayings that you mouth with your Tongues
Tongues are used to speak Words
Words are definitions of different Songs
Songs are heard through God's Hummingbirds.

Hummingbirds are winged animals of the Air
Air is unseen wind that you Feel
Feel is a slight touch that belongs There
There is where the heart is Real.

REJUVENATION: INNOCENT UNTIL PROVEN GUILTY

Stacey Barlow

Real is when something happens for you to think

"Okay"

Okay is fine and you're alright

Right is asking, Have you Given Thanks Today?

And Today will become a Peaceful Night

REJUVENATION: INNOCENT UNTIL PROVEN GUILTY

Stacey Barlow

REPETITION

Be Quiet! Shut out all the madness
It is Sad to turn a Deaf Ear
So don't do it More or Less
Include without Fear.

Open your Eyes
And See what's in front of you
Open your Arms
And Feel what's in front of you

Count the times you've heard
Realize the times you've seen
Dream the times you've missed
Don't do that please don't do this. . .

Raise your hands high
And praise God for your blessings
You should count
Yes, there are many. . . A hefty amount.

REJUVENATION: INNOCENT UNTIL PROVEN GUILTY

Stacey Barlow

Men call me Beauty

Men call me Sexy

Men say that I am Wife material

Men call me Intelligent

Men say that I am Unbelievable

Men call me Everything Good

But their own you see?

They. . .Just. . .Call. . .Me.

If you heard it once

You've heard it a thousand times over

With bright eyes that will spite Jehovah

I know my Body

I know my Mind

I know my Soul

Thanks to God I am Whole.

Thank you, Thank you, Thank you.

REJUVENATION: INNOCENT UNTIL PROVEN GUILTY

Stacey Barlow

MOUNTAIN

There is a Peak that I have to Reach
Along with a Lesson
THAT I HAVE TO TEACH.

If this Mountain is too High
You won't see the top
UNLESS YOU TRY.

If the River is too Wide to cross
Don't get discouraged
ALL IS **NOT** LOST.

At one time, we have all Failed
If you judge one then cast the First Stone
LET US SEE WHAT THEY TELL.

Nothing is Smooth, there is always a Rough Side
If someone said it was Easy
YOU TELL HIM HE LIED.

REJUVENATION: INNOCENT UNTIL PROVEN GUILTY

Stacey Barlow

I've climbed that Mountain
But Failed to reach the Top
I'm half way through my Mid-Life Crisis
SO THIS IS WHERE I MADE MY PIT STOP.

I figured the climb would be Tough
I looked up to See
How much further I had to go
I know that I only can depend on Me
And realized, I'M NOT STRONG ENOUGH.

I Inhaled and Exhaled as I said a Prayer
Then I realized, I had to keep going
I COULDN'T STAY THERE.

It felt like a long way, although it may seem
But I knew I had to keep climbing
THAT MOUNTAIN TO REACH MY DREAM.

REJUVENATION: INNOCENT UNTIL PROVEN GUILTY

Stacey Barlow

NOT A BROKEN DREAM

He made away for us
Before he Passed
The rights for you and me
Didn't Last.

The world should be color blind
All shades of Grey
This man had a Dream
He had something good to Say.

This man also had God on his side
That is the way
He kept his Pride.

He had a family just like you and I,
Little did he know
He had to say Goodbye.

REJUVENATION: INNOCENT UNTIL PROVEN GUILTY

Stacey Barlow

His words are memorably steadfast
"Free At Last, Free At Last
Thank God Almighty
I'm Free At Last."

The world is full of corruption
And all this worries me
It lets me know
We are not yet Free.

This he knew before he passed
That togetherness
Probably Wouldn't Last.

As far as we know
It is NOT a Broken Dream
We all should have one for the Future
Just like Dr. Martin Luther King Jr.

REJUVENATION: INNOCENT UNTIL PROVEN GUILTY

Stacey Barlow

LEARNING

If there is one thing I have Learned

While being with you;

The Lesson I have Learned

Is to keep Loving each other even when we're Angry.

REJUVENATION: INNOCENT UNTIL PROVEN GUILTY

Stacey Barlow

MS. CLASSIFIED

There was a young lady named Classie
She had Brown Eyes, Long Legs, Short Hair
And Sassy.

Men flocked and broke their necks
Trying to get to her
But once they did, their thoughts differed.

She was too good to be true
And she was as Sweet as a Rose
Why she turned so Bitter, nobody knows.

She met a man and married him,
Mr. Bona Fide was his name
They had two children
Twins--boy and a girl just the same.

REJUVENATION: INNOCENT UNTIL PROVEN GUILTY

Stacey Barlow

Dignified and Clarified
Both were the sweetest
As time went on
Their lives became a mess.

Ms. Classified was a woman
Who stood her ground
Even if her husband wasn't around.

Ms. Classified didn't take much
From men who broke her heart
Her mother taught her well
No man in her life, She doesn't want any part.

No, Ms. Classified is not a newspaper,
Written in ink
Ms. Classified is a woman who
Wants you to think

REJUVENATION: INNOCENT UNTIL PROVEN GUILTY

Stacey Barlow

Ms. Classified is a strong will inside of every woman

Who'll know how to stand her ground.

She has a message for every man around You:

Can

Let

A

Sister

Stay

In

Focus

If

Every Mr. Bona Fide lets you

Down

REJUVENATION: INNOCENT UNTIL PROVEN GUILTY

Stacey Barlow

MY VILLAGE

When it Rains

It Pours

But when the sun comes out

My people

Work together

As One

To

Build up

All

Happiness inside.

The ground always has

Flowers

To plant

And the skies. . .

REJUVENATION: INNOCENT UNTIL PROVEN GUILTY

Stacey Barlow

Air to breathe

When the sun

Goes down

It's time

To

Withdraw

From a days work.

My temple is clean

And MY VILLAGE is at rest.

REJUVENATION: INNOCENT UNTIL PROVEN GUILTY

Stacey Barlow

OCEAN'S TEARS

As the Sun sets and the Moon fall
Love grows by the Ocean's shore
As my calls cry out to you
TO COME BACK TO ME.

Hoping that the waves will carry this message safely
From my Mouth, to God's Ears, into your Heart
So that it may dwell
Deep inside a Soul that Stirs
Stirs with an undying feeling
So that I too may know
That your Heart is Healing.
Far away from mine eyes that can't see
Ears that can't hear but to
Only be Confident in knowing that waters
Between us can't Separate the Love that flows like a
Stream in our Spirit.

REJUVENATION: INNOCENT UNTIL PROVEN GUILTY

Stacey Barlow

My Heart shall not Fear

Because it is the way it should be

And though War should Rise against you

I hope that the waters

BRING YOU BACK TO ME.

Psalms 27:3

For the Troops

REJUVENATION: INNOCENT UNTIL PROVEN GUILTY

Stacey Barlow

SECOND INFINITY

Numbers one to three

Only carries as far as

You can count to ten

REJUVENATION: INNOCENT UNTIL PROVEN GUILTY

Stacey Barlow

SISTER ON THE RISE (THE ANSWER)

Say Baby, what can you do for me as my Slave?
I've got to claim you Boy
You're a shame Boy
You'll be digging your own Grave.

Daughter to the spinning post I may be
And Queen of 10,000 moons
Man, you must be High, talking that Smack
And Who is O'shoon?

It must not be me because that's not my name
What if I'm not ready to Play your Game?

Stand before me like a mystical god wet all over
Bring the pain Baby
Sing my name Baby
With a six pack that'll spite Jehovah.

REJUVENATION: INNOCENT UNTIL PROVEN GUILTY

Stacey Barlow

Who am I? It's not important
But they call me Sister on the Rise

And right now, I'm the Beat in your Heart
Trying to become the Jazz in your Eyes.

Who am I? I'm whomever you see
But right now, I'm the closure in your mind
And that's the way it should be.

I'm giving you injections of Divine Perfections
So you can dance to my Rhythms
Kaleidoscope paintings are the things
Of whispered secrets in circled rings

Upon wings of distorted metaphoric ciphers
Excuse me Sir
Fuck your woman--I ain't worried about her.

REJUVENATION: INNOCENT UNTIL PROVEN GUILTY

Stacey Barlow

You know I kind of like you steppin'
To me the way you do so
Deal with reality now while you're on the scene
Then maybe you won't wonder about romancing me
In a Wet Dream.

Who am I? Well, they call me Sister on the Rise
And right now, I am the Beat in your Heart
Trying to become the Jazz in your Eyes
Do you mind?

REJUVENATION: INNOCENT UNTIL PROVEN GUILTY

Stacey Barlow

WALK IN MY SHOES

As I turned the corner to my favorite shoe store
Ready to be adored
Screaming "Buy me, Buy me"
From the tips of their Tongues
I ached inside because I knew
They were the ones

So I skipped inside thinking that I could buy
Those famous pair
Even though I knew I couldn't afford to get them
Couldn't even afford to stare.

Those Shoes cried for me
And my Feet ached for them
I knew when putting them on Lay-a-way
Was even Very Slim.

REJUVENATION: INNOCENT UNTIL PROVEN GUILTY

Stacey Barlow

Oh My Goodness what have I done?
I ran up my Credit Card bill
Using Capitol One

That's it! I'll pull out my Discover card
That one is already High
Paying that off shouldn't be too Hard.

Whew! Okay I'm gonna get MY shoes
What? You don't say! The card was Declined
I just knew I wouldn't Lose.

I turned to put the shoes back
And man... Didn't that make me Sick
To walk out of Neiman Marcus without my
Manolo Blahnik's.

REJUVENATION: INNOCENT UNTIL PROVEN GUILTY

Stacey Barlow

REJUVENATION

Reason for me being here in this time is to not
Exist walking around in a daze trying to
Justify myself to people who
Use a tone of
Voice when speaking to me trying to
Earn a place in this
Natural life making it evident that it isn't
Always a smart idea living differently
Treating me with disrespect because
I am known to just exist
On a day to day basis
Now I am finally. . .Living

REJUVENATION: INNOCENT UNTIL PROVEN GUILTY

Stacey Barlow

Why I Support RAINN: I believe that getting help is the single most critical step a victim of sexual assault can take on the path to becoming a survivor. It is vital that victims have access to free and anonymous support services whenever needed. RAINN provides a safe outlet where victims and their friends and family can go to receive free, live and anonymous support around the clock. This organization means a lot to me and I hope that you will support my efforts to enable RAINN to help more victims. Let us help save lives.

Every two minutes, somewhere in America, someone is sexually assaulted. **One in six women** are victims of sexual assault, and *one in 33 men* About *44%* of rape victims are *under age 18*, and *80% are under age 30.*

PROVEN GUILTY

REJUVENATION: INNOCENT UNTIL PROVEN GUILTY

Stacey Barlow

REAL WOMEN/FAKE MEN

I know we just met
But you could have said something more
Than "Hey I wanna Kiss, Hug and Pet
My way through your shore."

We conversed and you related your Desire
To me to manipulate My Soul
Tearing me to Pieces
Waiting for me to wait on you
I shall, No More.

We share an Intimate thought
With Space and Time
And I even Breathe air to say
I want you to be Mine.

You ignored the friendly request

REJUVENATION: INNOCENT UNTIL PROVEN GUILTY

Stacey Barlow

Because you like so many
Real women are not a test
Stop living in the land of sent aplenty

My spirit is stirred with my number
I Wrote
You left feeling better
High above the sky
You tend to float
There was no Call
Or an Answer to be heard
I hope that you are seeing this and
Read every word.

I am Phenomenal and this is True
Once you find that none can compare
It will stop being all about you.

REJUVENATION: INNOCENT UNTIL PROVEN GUILTY

Stacey Barlow

I am Phenomenal as you will see
That out of all of "them"
I am REAL
So Get Ready, Get ready, Get ready
For Me

I'll put a different Stride in your Walk
And an unusual Bend in your back
You'll even change the way you Talk
This is so NOT Fiction
This is a Fact

Many a man have come to me
And told me what I am about
Not bragging because I don't have to
I'll just let you figure it out.

Down Right Dirty, you are

REJUVENATION: INNOCENT UNTIL PROVEN GUILTY

Stacey Barlow

And I will back away
Let's see if this thing will go far
And the question will be
Can you make me stay?

Players~play
But Real Women Rule
Fake Men won't get the time of day
You'll only get Schooled.
Learn your Lesson
Do what you have to do
I have no time for childish games
I think I've just schooled you

Do you want a Real Phenomenal woman?
Or do you still want to still play with toys?
It's time for your mind to be made up
I don't deal with Boys!

REJUVENATION: INNOCENT UNTIL PROVEN GUILTY

Stacey Barlow

Oh! One more thing (I'll repeat this)

I'll put a different Stride in your Walk
And an unusual Bend in your back
You'll even change the way you Talk
This is so NOT Fiction
This is a Fact.

REJUVENATION: INNOCENT UNTIL PROVEN GUILTY

Stacey Barlow

DELIVER ME (PSALMS 70)

Deliver me from my wicked ways

So that I might see better days

Deliver me and cleanse my soul

Deliver me and make me whole.

REJUVENATION: INNOCENT UNTIL PROVEN GUILTY

Stacey Barlow

DANGEROUS THOUGHTS

Have you ever wanted to Kill a man with your Bare Hands
Just because he Left you?
Or would you sit in the corner of your home
AND CRY A TIME OR TWO?

Have you ever wanted to Slap someone across the Face
Because he or she looked at you in a Strange way?
Or would you let him or her pass you by
AND TRY TO HAVE A NICE DAY?

Would you step on their Toes
Without saying Excuse Me
Or keep on walking
AS IF YOU DIDN'T SEE?

Would you Shoot someone
Knowing it was a Mistaken Identity?
Or would you keep telling the cops
"IT WASN'T ME! IT WASN'T ME!"

REJUVENATION: INNOCENT UNTIL PROVEN GUILTY

Stacey Barlow

Would you Stab someone
Leaving them to Die?
Just leaving them there
AND NOT ASKING YOURSELF, WHY?

Would you ever Kiss a man
And then, him, you Suffocate?
Lying in his Bed, taking his Last Breath
KNOWING FOR HIM, IT WAS TOO LATE?

Would you Hand a person over something he Bought?
And become Embarrassed because you Stole it
AND YOU GOT CAUGHT?

This is a scenario
If you want an answer, I decline.
The only thought I would give
IS IT REAL, OR IN THE MIND?

REJUVENATION: INNOCENT UNTIL PROVEN GUILTY

Stacey Barlow

WISH YOU WERE HERE (A DREAM OF 2PAC)

I walked into the doors of the place where you used to hang
All Eyes were on Me
Because the people knew I hadn't let you go
I didn't set you Free.

Coming in hearing about a Wishing Well
I had to try it out to bring you back
A Penny for your Thoughts
A Nickel for a Kiss
A Dime to hear you say you Love me
And a Quarter to make you Stay
Forever more.

I waited a while
And there was a knock at the side door
I went over and opened it and there you stood
I screamed in horror
"No it couldn't be!"
You said, "Yes, it could."

REJUVENATION: INNOCENT UNTIL PROVEN GUILTY

Stacey Barlow

You wanted me to step to the other side
As you motioned your hand my way
I moved back and you came to where I was
You put your arms around me
It felt so Real, not to mention Good.

I turned to face you
As you looked down at me and Smiled
Then you Kissed me and Held me
For a little while.

Every time I needed you, you had my back
And you set me Free
And the last words you whispered were. . .
"Thank you for wishing of me."

REJUVENATION: INNOCENT UNTIL PROVEN GUILTY

Stacey Barlow

BUT GOD (THE ICE BERRY CHRONICLES)

My friends call me Ice Berry
There is so much on my mind that needs to be said
And it may seem quite scary
Now God doesn't like liars, killers, stealers, cheaters
Including the unnatural act
But I'm here to say; I've done all of that.
I pulled up on a boy who had some nice kicks
But I only needed them to get a quick fix
He ran and I ran after him pumping his body
Full of lead--one in the back, two in the stomach
And three in the head.

But God seen what was being done
Same thing happened to me--I was paralyzed
And lived through it
Ice Berry--0, Father--1.

I did the dirty deed of fornicating through my temple
For me, getting a clean spirit isn't that simple.

REJUVENATION: INNOCENT UNTIL PROVEN GUILTY

Stacey Barlow

But God heard my cries
While lying in a hospital room
But, I was crying so loud that I didn't hear Him say,
"I am here for you."
Ice Berry--0, Son--2.

Come to find out while there,
I was going to have a little Shorty
But God whispered in my ear,
"Daughter you've been naughty."

I fell asleep
And someone appeared just to say,
"Let me make one thing clear,
you haven't been a good girl
so I'm going to leave you here."

I knew at that point I was given a chance
To show my Shorty
The better side of me
Ice Berry--1 but the Holy Ghost--3

REJUVENATION: INNOCENT UNTIL PROVEN GUILTY

Stacey Barlow

Since God entered into my life
Things haven't been the same
Yeah, my homies call me Ice Berry
But with God, I prefer my real name.

REJUVENATION: INNOCENT UNTIL PROVEN GUILTY

Stacey Barlow

BULLET PROOF

I thought he seen me coming up the alley
But I guess not

I looked to the skies for breath
But they refuse to lend a helping hand.

The air was hot against my skin
As I pulled upward toward the Heaven in a
Near miss situation

I floated as if to smell the aroma of
Jasmine and honey
MMM what a smell of therapeutic anointment as
My, My, My, MYYYYYYY

Soul drift through the clouds in finding
There was no one waiting for me

REJUVENATION: INNOCENT UNTIL PROVEN GUILTY

Stacey Barlow

OOOOOOO no one waited

While. . .

I heard a voice calming yet serene bringing my eyes

Back to their regular state

Convulsing, body shaking then slumped

The tear ducts let out a flow of salty water to my cheeks

Gasping for air I thought that I had lost myself in the

Midst of the

Confusion. . .

What happened?

I'll be fine

The man got away

Thinking that I wasn't

Bullet Proof.

REJUVENATION: INNOCENT UNTIL PROVEN GUILTY

Stacey Barlow

FEELING THE PAIN
(SUICIDE PASSION SECOND CHRONICLES)

Ice Berry, Ice Berry

Where did you go?

I saw you getting ready

To

Jump from a third floor window.

Ice Berry, Ice Berry

You'll be truly missed

I saw you getting ready

To

Use a knife on your wrist.

Ice Berry, Ice Berry

Please live to see the sun

If you leave this world

Who'll take care of your

Little one?

Ice Berry, Ice Berry

REJUVENATION: INNOCENT UNTIL PROVEN GUILTY

Stacey Barlow

Push it aside

Get on your knees

To pray

And let God guide.

Remember when

He took care of you?

He gave you a second chance

I thought you knew.

Ice Berry, Ice Berry

I opened the door

To hear a bang

I saw a chair and a rope

In which you hang.

If you did this

God won't forgive you

You're on your own.

Tell me who else do you think will miss you

If you're gone?

REJUVENATION: INNOCENT UNTIL PROVEN GUILTY

Stacey Barlow

CARRY ON

Did you see it?
I didn't I missed.

One shot to the head
My friend saw a man
Fall dead
Carry on.

Did you hear it?
I didn't, I missed it.

Cries of a woman
Being hit
Just because her man
Had a fit
Carry on.

Did you smell it?
I didn't, I missed.

REJUVENATION: INNOCENT UNTIL PROVEN GUILTY

Stacey Barlow

A body of an elderly
Lying on the floor
Curled up behind the bathroom door
Carry on.

Did you touch it?
I didn't, I missed it.

The bruises of a young one
Being punished
Just because a child was having fun
Carry on.

Did you taste it?
I didn't, I missed it.

The bitterness shot into skin
This is what the world is made up of
This violence must end
Carry on.

REJUVENATION: INNOCENT UNTIL PROVEN GUILTY

Stacey Barlow

GREEN-EYED DEVIL

That old green-eyed devil poked
His narrow nose into my business
And screwed everything that was beautiful
And divine in my Life.

I fell on love with this green-eyed devil just so that
He could take my Soul
And Burn it.

Somebody save me from this green-eyed devil who
Still torments me in the middle of the night
In the Morning and Noonday, I fight.

To keep my Sanity well in mind
That green-eyed devil will be hard to find
He will fight to win knowing your Weakness
You will Lose . . .
It's him, me, your Soul--
You have to Choose.

REJUVENATION: INNOCENT UNTIL PROVEN GUILTY

Stacey Barlow

On an easier note,
There is a struggle with every green-eyed devil
He's going to really burn you if you stoop to his level.

As you know that it level low; if you go that far
To be where he is; don't give him the opportunity
To beat you down, or he might just also get your kids.

Yes, I've stooped to his level only to beat him
That old green-eyed devil will be around for a Lifetime
If you're strong enough don't let your light go dim
Be happy in this case, killing him wouldn't be a Crime.

I don't like green-eyed devils
Because they won't tell the truth
The green-eyed devils can be some men in general
If this doesn't apply,
Then I'm not talking about you.

REJUVENATION: INNOCENT UNTIL PROVEN GUILTY

Stacey Barlow

LIPSTICK ON THE COLLAR (ASK ME)

You want to know the Real Deal
About the Lipstick on the Collar
All you had to do was dial the number in his pocket
And give me a Hollah

He's only out to get away from you
Cursing and carrying on
Let him come in at 2. . .

If he wants, he can stay the night
At my house plus
Sleep in my Bed
And not on the Couch
Stop sweating a Brothah
About color on his collar

As I said before
Check the number in his pocket
And give me a Hollah.

REJUVENATION: INNOCENT UNTIL PROVEN GUILTY

Stacey Barlow

Oh and about the fake nails and bad hair
That was also your sister he was
Hollering at, she too was there.

So you see, it's not just me
It's Tasha, Tanisha, Tameka

From around the way
Get your stuff together
And Have a Nice Day.

Instead of asking him about his shirt
Why don't I just tell him that you too
Have also been digging dirt.

I seen you the other day
Hugged up in the grocery store
With a guy named James,
Oh Yeah! I seen you,
That's my uncle's son

REJUVENATION: INNOCENT UNTIL PROVEN GUILTY

Stacey Barlow

So now who's playing games?
What about the time
You were riding some dude in your car
Then turned down 54th street
I see you didn't get very far.

What about the day I seen you in the Park
You were Screaming so loud
You were making the Dogs Bark.

Naw I ain't peepin' you
Just looking out for what's really mine
So the next collar you see Lipstick on
The color, Coffee Bean
And my name is Sunshine

So don't go asking about the Lipstick on his Collar
Just look for the number in his left pants pocket
And give me a Hollah.

REJUVENATION: INNOCENT UNTIL PROVEN GUILTY

Stacey Barlow

Oh yeah the loving we made was on point I must admit

And the next time to see lipstick on the collar

Don't ask

JUST WASH IT. . .

REJUVENATION: INNOCENT UNTIL PROVEN GUILTY

Stacey Barlow

LIPSTICK ON THE COLLAR (PART II)

I know she didn't just hang up on me

Dialing#. 3333

Look here Ms. Forgotten

Yes, I am talking to you

Let me set you straight

Before I have to turn you

Black and Blue

I tried to be civilized

As a woman should

And tell you where your man

Is taking his wood.

That's right

I called out names

Because James has a Big Mouth

That's how I know your business

I even know where you live

Down South.

REJUVENATION: INNOCENT UNTIL PROVEN GUILTY

Stacey Barlow

You can have that man
I don't want your Leftovers anyway
And the only reason he came to me
Is because he said
You don't even cook
On any Given Day

I heard about the steak as well
Heard you were Burned
He went to the clinic
And guess what he Learned?

So, you need to go back
To your man and get the Truth
Better yet, call your cousin
You know the one, her name is Ruth.

Oh yeah, she's in that clique along with
The rest of us
Tanya, Tia, Shannon...
Need I say more?

REJUVENATION: INNOCENT UNTIL PROVEN GUILTY

Stacey Barlow

Or have you heard enough?
Yeah I did say to Hollah
Because I'm tired of his sh*t
Running back to me
Every time you two have
An argument.

Disturbing the Peace
WTF do you mean?
Ya'll fussing and fighting all the time
That man needs to come clean.

So there you have it, I'll
Forever be up in your mix
You better get that story straight
Or have him to get something fixed.

Oh no! Wait! So this means
He is really not yours
And if you want to fight about it
Then we can step outdoors.

REJUVENATION: INNOCENT UNTIL PROVEN GUILTY

Stacey Barlow

I'm not one for busting caps
In anybody's Ass
But this time I will make an exception
Woman, I'm from his Past

That night we just got caught up
One time only
So, Hell No! I'm nowhere near lonely

There are plenty of men out there
But I wanted him
As you can see I got what I wanted
Plus you and them.

He keeps coming back to
My Front Door
You must not be doing something right
Because I had him lying on the Floor.

If you're bold enough
Come and get him

REJUVENATION: INNOCENT UNTIL PROVEN GUILTY

Stacey Barlow

But you won't find him here
He's around the corner
Screwing Chantel
He has been doing that since Last Year.

See what you failed to realize is that
I'll be forever in his life
Did he forget to mention
That I was his first wife?

So, let's just squash the color on the collar
I just wanted to call you back
And get things straight
And if you still want to. . .
Hollah

REJUVENATION: INNOCENT UNTIL PROVEN GUILTY

Stacey Barlow

CONVERSATION

Hello, is this Ebony

Nice to speak to you

Well, let me tell you

From the beginning

What I did do

First off

I never said I didn't like Donna's ways

Because Clarence treated her good

That was up until he heard

She had another man up in the hood.

I didn't lie about the time

Spent with Ant

I couldn't put up with his trifling ways

Still won't...CAN'T

You must be one I missed

Or didn't know of

REJUVENATION: INNOCENT UNTIL PROVEN GUILTY

Stacey Barlow

I see you have five years of him
And all his love

Don't get me wrong
I don't do what he says I do
I own my own poetry business
I just wish he'd stop
Telling lies
And clean up his mess.

So now I guess he's going back and forth
Between each woman
I wonder does he know
How much we all can stand
Clarence is my boy, blood and
Always will be
And what he says is the truth
And thankful that he took up for me

But I don't agree that Donna
Is a whore

REJUVENATION: INNOCENT UNTIL PROVEN GUILTY

Stacey Barlow

We had a decent conversation last night
After their steak
And she really doesn't need that anymore

You know Ant said the same thing to me
About carrying his seed
I'm glad that I didn't go through with it
That would have been a father
That child didn't need.

I'm too old for games
And I felt I could make
Him a better man
I thought wrong
That was the decision
On the other hand
Hmm, so yours was
The lipstick I found
On his collar
I thought nothing of it as first
Glad we got a chance to Hollah

REJUVENATION: INNOCENT UNTIL PROVEN GUILTY

Stacey Barlow

I'm not one for running rumors
Or playing games
Do what you will if you must
Call James

Trust me, my cuz is a sensitive
Cat
He's more of a romantic
He likes it like that.
Oh! By the word
Here's the number to my cell
Just dial that

If you have something else to tell
Women don't need a man
Like Ant in our lives
We deserve the best
And then maybe you
I and Donna can get together
And put that dead head to rest

REJUVENATION: INNOCENT UNTIL PROVEN GUILTY

Stacey Barlow

GUESS WHO'S . . .

Oh! Gettin' Scured

Just cause you got

Your so called Lady

On the Phone

But what he didn't tell you Donna

Was that he called me last night

Wantin' to Bone

Don't lie about what you Feel

That was after High School

When we got Married

So YOU keep it Real

Hard luck my Ass

When you settled on court

I got cold hard Cash

REJUVENATION: INNOCENT UNTIL PROVEN GUILTY
Stacey Barlow

So I'm not down on it
You're the one who's struggling
But you just remember this
Who'd you come to
When you needed the money

For your Bitch's ring?
And what about that car you driving
That's in my name
I'm taking my name off that lease
And let you pay for it
For a change

I don't wear wigs
My hair is real baby
What you need to do
Is fix up your so called
New Lady

REJUVENATION: INNOCENT UNTIL PROVEN GUILTY

Stacey Barlow

With her Mary J, Free looking
P*ssy totin' antics
Gonna try and ruffle my Feathers
Both your behinds make me Sick!

Why you want to lie to her
Is beyond My Control
Now you got Sarah calling my house
You'd never guess what she told?

She saw you Mr. Man
On 54th street giving head
And that it wasn't a woman
Actually a husky dude with dreads
So before you go yapping at the mouth
About whoever else
You don't claim to be with
Fuck the Lipstick on the Collar

REJUVENATION: INNOCENT UNTIL PROVEN GUILTY
Stacey Barlow

That's your shirt

You wash it.

You got me twisted

That was you drinking

I don't touch the stuff

You're the one didn't want to go home that night

What were you thinking?

Your girl Donna, peeped you

The night you went to Dee's

She had front row seats

Just outside

Hearing you beggin' please.

How did she know about that?

I drove her there

You can't talk about nobody's bad hair.

REJUVENATION: INNOCENT UNTIL PROVEN GUILTY

Stacey Barlow

Thought you were better when you picked them
But I guess not
You just mad because you got caught

But don't look my way for answers
Because they are right there
In front of your face
I'm glad I'm not married to your
Sorry Ass anymore

So you can keep me out of your rat race.
That's your mouth saying I hoe just to get paid
At least that's good money
And what do you do?
Low grade wanna be
So and so
No money making
Hospital aide.

REJUVENATION: INNOCENT UNTIL PROVEN GUILTY

Stacey Barlow

As for you Little Miss forgotten

Looks like you still need to come clean

Instead of continuing to

Talk to me

Call the other women and talk to them

Nah I mean?

If you look in his glove compartment

You'll find more than one digit

You'll even find your best friend's number there

Bridgette.

I guess my Brotah, I still love Ya

But you still have oats

You're sowing

Pick up your face donkey breath

And tell me now

Who's doing the hoeing?

REJUVENATION: INNOCENT UNTIL PROVEN GUILTY

Stacey Barlow

CONFERENCE CALL

Ladies!
He must have been
Fooling around with all of us
At the Same Time

Yo!
I'm telling you
Let's neuter this Dog
He's got to Go.

Remember now I was his First wife
I apologize Donna for saying
I'd Forever be in his Life

Chantel, now I know
It was more than just a Fling
I saw the receipt from
Gordon's Jewelers
A 3.5 Karat Diamond Ring.

REJUVENATION: INNOCENT UNTIL PROVEN GUILTY

Stacey Barlow

Donna, you might not get much
From the Divorce settlement
That was all given to me
And the Poetry business I have
Is where that money went.

I won't be stingy Donna
I'll share with you what I received
And help your children through school if you want
And help you get what you wish to Achieve

That's too much Money for me
To just keep for myself
I did give Clarence some of my earnings
And I think he gave Ebony
What he had left.

Chantel, you can Pawn that Ring
Or give it to your sister Hazel
I know that ring is worth a lot
Found out from the jewelry appraisal.

REJUVENATION: INNOCENT UNTIL PROVEN GUILTY

Stacey Barlow

Seeing that we've come to the conclusion
Of all that is learned

Please ladies have a Good Night
And God speed

Give me a call, if you need me
Meeting adjourned.

REJUVENATION: INNOCENT UNTIL PROVEN GUILTY

Stacey Barlow

CONCLUSION

Kneel Brothah!

Drop to your knees

Stay your ass on the floor

And beg a Sistah please

Ah Hell Naw they won't lock me up

Because I'm claiming

Self defense

For once and for all

I'm gonna End this. . .

With your two double line

Rhyming Fat Ass

You need to take a Lesson

From an English teacher

And go back to Class

You misread me see

I wouldn't have

REJUVENATION: INNOCENT UNTIL PROVEN GUILTY

Stacey Barlow

A child by you
The First One I didn't
Tell you about
It was a Miscarriage
Because you Beat me

That ain't Cool.
I've got friends all over the world

Wanna know how?
It's not what you say
So how you like me now?

Uh Uh Uuuh don't even try it
Don't you move One Inch of your Bones

I'm gonna make sure
You never use that thing again
And that you won't have not one
Loves Jones.

REJUVENATION: INNOCENT UNTIL PROVEN GUILTY

Stacey Barlow

You trying to be all Hard
And not Twitch
But I know for a fact that
Brian, Jason, Damon, and Al
Had you crying like a little Bitch.

That's right Ladies
That's why I dropped kicked his Butt
I caught him in the bed with Jason
Hittin it from the back
What! What!

Ahh man I wish
You would open your mouth
To Speak
I just wanna make you feel
That Steel

On the front of your teeth
I'd put a Bullet so far up your behind
You'd feel the Freeze

REJUVENATION: INNOCENT UNTIL PROVEN GUILTY

Stacey Barlow

WHAT?! DOG WHAT?!
I want to hear you say it
N**** say please.

I'm more woman than
You'll ever have again
I don't care how many times
You mess with the others
Bald, Fat, Broke or Thin.

I got a right mind to
Blow your head away
And not feel Bad about what I did
And write a story about it
Now let's see what you gotta say

Huh? I. . .
Can't. . .
Heeeeeear. . .
Yooooooou. . .
Speak up

REJUVENATION: INNOCENT UNTIL PROVEN GUILTY

Stacey Barlow

You're
Whis-per-ing
I bet you if
I shoot you now
Would I hear you Sing?

Laughing evilly
I thought so
Why are you sweating?
Scured still?
Did you think I would let you go?

And get away with
Spreading bad things about me
Around town?

Well, let me hip you
To a few new things
You didn't know about me
This is how I get down?

REJUVENATION: INNOCENT UNTIL PROVEN GUILTY

Stacey Barlow

What you didn't know

Was that my Uncle is in

The Mafia

And yes I told him

What you been doing.

How do you think I got what I got

While you were out Screwing?

So as you can see

The jail thing you mention

And the job at the Retail store

I was just waiting

For you to screw up

And you put your Foot in the Door.

All the Ladies that have been

Dialing my number

Since day one

Owes my Uncle favors

You've just made the case

The damage is Done.

REJUVENATION: INNOCENT UNTIL PROVEN GUILTY

Stacey Barlow

The favor was
To keep an eye out for you
Because I thought
You might have been skank
My assumptions were right
I had you tailed
Now whatcha thank?

Oh No! I'm not finished with you yet
So stay on your Knees
You will finally hear me out
If it takes hours
Or until your Legs Bleed.

I was the one who took you in
When your trifling behind
Was out in the cold
You ain't so young yourself
Trying to be hip Papa Daddy
Your broke behind
Is old.

REJUVENATION: INNOCENT UNTIL PROVEN GUILTY

Stacey Barlow

Do you want to get up now
Or do you want to live
Would you like to spit fire at me?
And tell me how much you can give.

I'm tired of wasting
Unwanted breath on you
Because you can't seem
To get the hint
I came
I saw
I conquered
I went.

Today I digress
You still have oats
You've sown
Now tell me
Do you want to die
Or do you want to go home?

REJUVENATION: INNOCENT UNTIL PROVEN GUILTY

Stacey Barlow

THE END

I'm not giving up

Without a fight

Ant I'll deal with you later

Ebony, B*tch--Good Night

BANG! BANG! BANG!

Undercover you're just

A Toy Cop

Waiving around a pistol

For fun Naw I ain't Crazy, nor a Hoe

Now do Ya'll Ladies want some?

It was going to be a civilized meeting

And I can put my gat

Down as well

But I swear if that man

Comes near me

I'm going to give him more hell

REJUVENATION: INNOCENT UNTIL PROVEN GUILTY

Stacey Barlow

Ebony I thought we were
In this together up
In this place
I'm not really dangerous

I told Ya'll to leave me
Out of this rat race
No jail time for me
I'll make that bail
Ant I'll always love you
And the others will too
more than you could ever tell.

I said I will end this
And that I will do
No one will ever take my life
Just because I had it in for you.

Get up off the floor you Clown
You know in my Heart I will
Never shoot you down.

REJUVENATION: INNOCENT UNTIL PROVEN GUILTY

Stacey Barlow

Ebony you can get up Now

There were fake bullets in the gun

And it's all over

Ant do you think

You've learned your lesson,

Now go back to your lover.

GOTCHA!

REJUVENATION: INNOCENT UNTIL PROVEN GUILTY
Stacey Barlow

TICK TICK BOOM (WOOOSAAAAH MOMENT)

I laid into him like a mattress
And grilled him like cheese
"Oh please Baby Baby please"

I suggest that you understand
My wants and my needs
To fulfill my every fantasy that she was given to me
WOOOOSAAAH

I was going to tell you eventually
Eventually?

So you're saying that if I hadn't asked you wouldn't
Have told me about your dirty deed
And hoping you can come back to me
And fill me with your nasty greed
And think that everything would be fine between you and me
WOOOOSAAAH

REJUVENATION: INNOCENT UNTIL PROVEN GUILTY

Stacey Barlow

You got me twisted Shrek
And then had the audacity to say you
Didn't want to get her upset
What the heck?!

A complete stranger at that
What were you thinking?
WOOOOSAAAH

You had me fooled I must admit
Telling me one thing
I hope she was worth it
Worth my time
My energy
My heart
And my spirit

It's funny though
So I'll say it again
You had me fooled I must admit
Telling me one thing

REJUVENATION: INNOCENT UNTIL PROVEN GUILTY

Stacey Barlow

WOOOOSAAAH

I sure hope she was worth it.

You jeopardized a friendship

For an uncommon piece

A total stranger at that

OH PLEASE!!!!!

I laid into him like a mattress

And grilled him like cheese

Then he called because of a guilty conscience

To try to put his mind at ease

WOOOOSAAAH

The last thing I said just to let him know

You cannot be trusted

So I'm letting you go

WOOOOSAAAH

REJUVENATION: INNOCENT UNTIL PROVEN GUILTY

Stacey Barlow

WHAT DID I SAY?

Didn't I tell you people to leave me alone?
But that's not in my nature
But I'll tell you be gone

I left this world and came back to haunt
I'm in a female body now
And you know what she wants

I'm trapped in a body that ain't even mine
So this PMS crap is kicking my behind

Okay so now I like the way I look
You should have seen my broke @$$ before
I wasn't the last of the litter
But the women literally knocked down my door
(To get away that is)
Maybe it was because of my. . . .
We won't say for sure
But I'll show you mine if you show me yours.

REJUVENATION: INNOCENT UNTIL PROVEN GUILTY

Stacey Barlow

I guess you didn't hear me the first time when I said

Get off my guns

What did I. . .

Stupid Ass Youngins.

I don't feel like talking so

Go do some floors

N****s tryin' to cop on a Brothah

But I bet my dick is bigger than yours.

What did I say?

REJUVENATION: INNOCENT UNTIL PROVEN GUILTY

Stacey Barlow

SHOCK TO THE SYSTEM

If it had not been for that angel
Who protected me through the night
I would have died in my bed
Crying to make it right

Oh say can you see
My eyes were blinded by
Femtality to show me the way
Of the world and how they are
To me.
Turn away again, my back's
Against the wall
My guardian angel did hear me when I called.

I invoke thee archangel Michael
I invoke thee archangel Gabriel
I invoke thee archangel Raphiel
I invoke thee archangel Uriel
Give me the strength, the love

REJUVENATION: INNOCENT UNTIL PROVEN GUILTY

Stacey Barlow

The healing to dwell

In this world that is so full of

Hatred and lies that men

Look you right in your face

And tell you that you are beautiful

But on the inside

You're slowly going back into your shell

Slapped in the face with words back at me

Stabbed in the back by

So called friends

Who thought I couldn't see

Punched in the stomach

For having a voice

They gouged out my eyes

For making my choice

What a shock to the system

Like de je vu before

Dear Heavenly Father

Take away this pain

Because I don't wanna be here anymore

REJUVENATION: INNOCENT UNTIL PROVEN GUILTY

Stacey Barlow

REJUVENATION

Reason for me being here in this time is to not

Exist walking around in a daze trying to

Justify myself to people who

Use a tone of

Voice when speaking to me trying to

Earn a place in this

Natural life making it evident that it isn't

Always a smart idea living differently

Treating me with disrespect because

I am known to just exist

On a day to day basis

Now I am finally. . .Living.

REJUVENATION: INNOCENT UNTIL PROVEN GUILTY

Stacey Barlow

REJUVENATION: INNOCENT UNTIL PROVEN GUILTY

Stacey Barlow

ADDICTION

I breathe you Baby

I take you in and

Inhale you

Choking on the essence of the Smoke

You Kissed into my Lungs

Your Smoke is your Love

You gave me

The night before

And I was so

High that

I didn't want to come

Down

I floated with that

Pleasure of seeing you again

And tasting the Sweetness

Of the Lips that

Is my drug of Choice

I love experiencing you

REJUVENATION: INNOCENT UNTIL PROVEN GUILTY

Stacey Barlow

And I don't want to Stop
Taking you because of the
Way you make me Feel.

All up in my Nose
Both my Arms
And between my Toes

In my Knees and in my Thighs
Even in the clothes I wear
People may not really realize
They would just have to be there
You make me High
With Desire
And Sexy in my Body
All the way through
This Drug makes me
Toss and turn all night
The Drug is
The man I Love
My Addiction is YOU

REJUVENATION: INNOCENT UNTIL PROVEN GUILTY
Stacey Barlow

PUNANY RITUAL

On warm nights when I think of you to the point of a whisper taking
You all inside of me, a feeling of moistness of one spirit you come to
Me in a dream as the phone rings I pick up the handle to whisper a
Sweet hello trying to catch my breath as if to say, "You're needed."

Help me to wonder where the soul lies as my eyes cry tears of joy
Hearing your voice among many over-stepping our boundaries as we
Fall, fall, fall, fall deep into the Punany spell of cosmic mystery and
Delight, delight, delight, delight with movement faster than a bullet
From a gun I have a taste of sweet Punany Ritual every night before.
Going to sleep, deep sleep, sleep deep as I drift off to my body, loving

Every inch of what my mama bears me with as a vessel, she made me
Created me gave me my Punany Ritual hours into the night, silent
Breaths are taken to ensure a safe journey to a land never forgotten
Don't stop the flow keep it going as only you know bring it down to
An end we have to finish because when we give into the power of the
Ritual that's when we can stop and feel the magic.

REJUVENATION: INNOCENT UNTIL PROVEN GUILTY

Stacey Barlow

THIS PIECE DOES NOT BELONG TO YOU…

I carried the weight of the world on my shoulders
My Brotah for you
Only to have it feel like a ton of bricks
Bending me over
Buckling my knees
Breaking me down just to
Build me up
And say "I am yours"
This piece

P-I-E-C-E
Does not belong to…
Whether you believe it or not
This Piece

P-I-E-C-E
Is mine to keep
And when I Give it
You'll Know it

REJUVENATION: INNOCENT UNTIL PROVEN GUILTY

Stacey Barlow

When you Know it
You'll Feel it
When you Feel it
You'll See that this Piece

P-I-E-C-E
Does not belong to "her" meaning
Having Every Right
For you to abuse what Piece

P-I-E-C-E
Does to Ease the Pain
My Mind, Body, Soul
And Spirit was given to you
Piece by Piece by Piece

P-I-E-C-E
To dwell in your domain
Like a slave without a cause
To be Free
Your Love is Poison

REJUVENATION: INNOCENT UNTIL PROVEN GUILTY

Stacey Barlow

I died to be Reborn again

Only to serve what the Fire has

Brought inside of me like the Phoenix

Rising to the sun to Burn

And watch over you for

500 more years

And if you want this Piece

P-I-E-C-E

You have to go

Through

My inner Peace

P-E-A-C-E to get it

This Piece

P-I-E-C-E

Does not belong to you,

You

You

You

You

REJUVENATION: INNOCENT UNTIL PROVEN GUILTY

Stacey Barlow

NINE LIVES

9~Cat on a hot tin roof aching
To jump down and be free with

8~Lives left to play with to
Walk around clawing at each and every

7~Signs that are left in the bended
Bones that are so hard to break while
There are

6~Days only to whist out the game
Of a mouse chase that is
Forbidden in
The cat's eye
Green
With envy

5~O'clock time to change the linens
On the bed because

REJUVENATION: INNOCENT UNTIL PROVEN GUILTY

Stacey Barlow

Cat has been bad

Tearing holes in sheets

Clawing again~Repeats

Because

She cat

Is hungry

4~Life and thirst for Freedom

At the hands of

Its owner, to pounce

From craving

The yarn that is

Entwined within the

Claws of her being

3~Times the Charm

As it begins again

2~Boggle the Brain

And make she cat

Turn the other way

REJUVENATION: INNOCENT UNTIL PROVEN GUILTY

Stacey Barlow

To walk the walk only she can walk

Just to be Free

1~Last time before she gives up

The Ghost

Black cat nine lives short days long nights

Living on the edge not afraid to die

Heartbeat's real strong but not for long

Better watch your step

Or you're gonna die.

Note: The very last stanza are lyrics from Janet Jackson's song "Black Cat"

REJUVENATION: INNOCENT UNTIL PROVEN GUILTY

Stacey Barlow

ABOUT THE AUTHOR:

Residing in Texarkana, Texas, Stacey is continuing to write until her heart is content. Stacey has been heard on different poetry shows on Blog talk Radio. She is presently working on her third and fourth project. Published a piece in "The Head Doctor Presents Punany: The Hip Hop Psalms III, The Onliners Erotic Poems, and Short Stories from People Just Like You" entitled "Punany Ritual" in 2005.

In 2008, Stacey wrote a play "Hands of Betrayal" in hopes that it will become a worldwide success. Stacey also plans to travel in the near future.

Praises For Rejuvenation: Innocent Until Proven Guilty

"This book represents the voice of today's young woman"

Jeff Rivera -
Bestselling Author of FOREVER MY LADY

www.ingramcontent.com/pod-product-compliance
Lightning Source LLC
Chambersburg PA
CBHW051436290426
44109CB00016B/1586